NAVAJO WEAVING HANDBOOK

A
MUSEUM OF NEW MEXICO PRESS
GUIDEBOOK

NAVAJO WEAVING HANDBOOK

Compiled by the Editors of
EL PALACIO MAGAZINE
with an Introduction by Nancy Fox

MUSEUM OF NEW MEXICO PRESS

FIRST EDITION

Copyright © 1974, 1977 by the Museum of New Mexico Press
Post Office Box 2087, Santa Fe, New Mexico 87503

ISBN: 0-89013-092-2
Library of Congress Catalog Card Number 77-74888

A note on the spelling: Both *Navajo* and *Navaho* are correct. The name was first put into written form by the early Spanish explorers, and this original spelling was "Navajo." In past decades, some scholars Anglicized the spelling to "Navaho," although the most recent trend has been to the traditional spelling. The Navajo Tribe itself uses the "jo" style, and it is preferred by the Museum of New Mexico and most other institutions. However, in this book you will find both spellings; we have elected to accept the original choice of the individual writers.

The examples of Navajo weaving that illustrate this book are from the collections of the Museum of New Mexico, the School of American Research collections in the Museum of New Mexico, and the Indian Arts Fund collections of the School of American Research.

Color photography by Art Taylor.
Book design by Betsy James.

CONTENTS

INTRODUCTION

From the inception of the weaver's craft among the Navajo, probably sometime after the mid-seventeenth century, it has represented a vital economic factor and certainly one of the outstanding artistic achievements of this gifted people. And though it has encountered vicissitudes, notably during the forced resettlement at Bosque Redondo and immediately thereafter, it has proved enduring, changing in response to changing demands, flourishing today as it did some two hundred years ago.

This handbook, compiled from a series of papers first published in the Museum of New Mexico's journal, *El Palacio,* undertakes a brief but wide ranging reconnaissance of the craft. Katherine Luomala's history of Navajo weaving—inextricable from the history of the Navajo themselves—incorporates highlights from Charles Avery Amsden's *Navaho Weaving,* still the most useful compendium of knowledge available upon the subject. Bertha Dutton, drawing upon years of experience first as Curator of Ethnology at the Museum of New Mexico and then as Director of the Museum of Navaho Ceremonial Art, has carried the record beyond Amsden's day to describe current regional styles. In addition, she has provided the potential buyer with some basic advice— the most important, it is worth repeating, being to please one's own taste above all.

Josephine Wapp, who was for many years an instructor in weaving at the Institute of American Indian Arts, explains the technology of the craft. And Sally and Lisa Kandarian, in their profile of Mabel O'Dell, explore a topic of special importance to collectors of older specimens: how Navajo textiles are repaired by the foremost expert in this field.

Lately, due to current demand and resultant skyrocketing prices —so different from the days when rugs were sold by the pound— the market has seen an influx of imitation Navajo textiles. Therefore the handbook is completed with Noel Bennet's section which furnishes methods of distinguishing a genuine Navajo rug.

These diverse articles, then, together constitute a broad introduction to the subject of Navajo weaving. Few terms of possible interest to the reader have been omitted. In regard to the varieties of textiles discussed, brief mention might also be made of a type called "wedge-weave" or "pulled warp." Woven primarily around the last decades of the nineteenth century, wedge-weaves were never produced in quantity, but exist in sufficient numbers to warrant the interest of collectors. They display a pattern consisting of zones of multicolored zig-zag stripes. Their peculiarity lies in the fact that the weaver, to simplify her task, has built up uneven areas, following the lines of the zig-zag design rather than carrying each row straight across from edge to edge. As a result, the weft is battened diagonally, pulling the warp in varying directions and creating a typically wavy-edged textile.

In this single respect, therefore, the term "wedge-weave" might be considered in connection with the term "lazy line"—the result of another time saving expedient. This typical feature of Navajo textiles occurs when the weaver builds up one area before changing position and moving across to the next. (Unlike wedge-weave, however, each individual area is battened at right angles to the warp, so no distortion is evident.)

Finally, "Yei" and "sandpainting" rugs both receive mention. It might be well, then, to reiterate that religious symbolism was not a traditional feature of Navajo weaving, but was grafted upon the craft and flourishes today in response to commercial demand. The development of such rugs might best be regarded in the broader context of "pictorial" textiles—which preceded them and which continue to enjoy great popularity. The pictorial style, in infancy, can be traced as far back as 1864, but came into prominence around 1880, incorporating an array of non-ceremonial depictions: objects ranging from railroad trains to the American flag, animal and human figures, and even highly realistic landscapes. And it was only after the turn of the century that designs and beings of ceremonial significance were also portrayed. (Pictorial rugs are covered in Charlene Cerny's *Navajo Pictorial Weaving*, published by the Museum of New Mexico.)

In the following pages, the reader will become familiar with many other elements which together make up the story of Navajo weaving.

Nancy Fox
Curator of the
Anthropology Collections,
Museum of New Mexico

NAVAJO
WEAVING:
A
HISTORY

The colorful woolen rugs and the silver and turquoise jewelry created by the Navaho have made the name of this tribe a household word among the American people. Neither silversmithing nor the weaving of wool is old in Navaho history; both developed in post-Spanish times. In a short period, however, the Navaho transformed them from crafts into fine arts. What is more remarkable to artists is that the Navaho have made their arts economically successful. The two arts did not develop contemporaneously among the Navaho. Weaving is almost two centuries older than silversmithing, for whereas the latter dates from about 1850, weaving began in the late seventeenth century, getting under way about the time of the Pueblo Rebellion of 1680. It is fairly certain that the Pueblos taught the Navaho to weave and that the Mexicans were their teachers in silverwork. But according to a Navaho myth, it was two legendary beings, Spider Man and Spider Woman, who taught them to weave.

In the American Southwest the weaving of wool and silversmithing originated through Spanish influence, Coronado's arrival fixing 1540 as the earliest date for the beginning of the crafts. This point is particularly interesting because long before Europeans came to the New World, beautiful metal work and weaving, which rank with the finest in the world, were developed in northern and western South America and to a lesser extent in Central America.

The weaving done by the Indians north of Mexico was likewise more primitive than that of the South American Indians, although

By Katherine Luomala

Examples of early weaving by Southwestern Indians are shown at right. Two early Pueblo headbands (carrying bands) are depicted in drawing at lower left. Prehistoric Basketmaker period sandal fragment from Arizona is at far right. (Drawings by Kenneth Chapman.)

13

almost every tribe from the northwest coast of North America to the Southwest had weaving of a kind. Some areas produced beautifully designed blankets from the hair of bisons or mountain goats. Naturally such blankets were not common since one first had to catch the bison or the mountain goat–not an easy task with primitive weapons. Tribes with even a very simple culture knew how to prepare and plait rabbit skins into warm robes. The Southwestern tribes, including the Navaho, also used yucca fiber and cedar bark to weave squares for crude blankets and clothing. The Pueblos even cultivated cotton and wove it on looms of the kind still used today by both Navaho and Pueblo weavers for wool.

When the Spanish came into the Southwest, lured by fantastic myths of the golden cities of Cibola, the Pueblo were doing fine work in cotton and creating delicate mosaics of turquoise. As the result of Spanish suggestion or tutelage, the Pueblos made their first attempts at weaving sheep wool. By 1680, when the Pueblos were gathering their forces in a final effort to oust their Spanish conquerors, the weaving of wool was well established as a tribal craft. Many of the Pueblo dwellers fled to the Navaho wilderness for refuge. It is believed that these refugees taught the Navaho to weave.

Amsden's masterly book, *Navaho Weaving,* traces the history of this craft, which is also the history of the Navaho. Two paragraphs (p. 133) summarize the development of weaving during the late eighteenth and the early nineteenth centuries: "Of these four earliest known references to Navaho weaving (Spanish documents), each is more definite and emphatic than its predecessor. Croix in 1780 merely mentions the Navaho as weavers. Chacon in

Bold, contrasting stripes are set off by terraced diamond pattern in the weave of this classic "chief" blanket. Men of many tribes once wore Navajo shoulder blankets of this type with understandable pride.

1795 concedes them supremacy over the Spaniards in 'delicacy and taste' in weaving. Cortez in 1799 makes it clear that the production of blankets more than suffices for tribal needs. Pino in 1812 categorically places Navaho weaving at the head of the textile industry in three large provinces: significantly ahead even of the Pueblo craft, which mothered that of the Navaho.

"On abundant evidence then, the Navaho had gained a recognized supremacy in native Southwestern weaving in wool as early as the opening of the 19th century; and down to the present day that supremacy has never been relinquished. The Hopi craftsman may have shown more conscience and conservatism at certain times, but the Navaho women have proved the more versatile, imaginative and progressive, and the Navaho blanket has always been the favored child of that odd marriage of the native American loom with the fleece of European sheep."

Amsden (p. 223) distinguishes two definite cycles in the history of Navaho weaving: the intra-tribal or native, and the commercial or transition ("the era of the reservation and the trading post"). He states: "Each rested upon an economic basis and was molded by and to the needs of the time—for this is a craft, an industry, and like all such its existence depends on a human want." In addition to these two cycles, Amsden indicates that, although "this (second) phase is still (1934) in full vigor, yet there are signs of an impending readjustment to the changing times." This readjustment he calls the Revival, and dates it from 1920.

The native period dates from the beginning of Navaho weaving in wool, when they wove clothes and blankets for tribal use only, and continues until that time during the late eighteenth century

Another classic "chief" blanket, in white, brown, blue and red (55" x 65"). Weavings shown on these pages are from the collections of the School of American Research and the Museum of New Mexico.

when they began to weave for neighboring tribes and the Spanish. The weavers spun the natural, undyed sheep wool of black, gray, brown, and white and wove the yarn into designs of plain stripes of varying widths. The most characteristic product was a two-piece dress for women. Some of the finest weaving ever to be achieved by the Navaho women was produced in this intra-tribal period, when the weavers toiled only to satisfy their high standards of workmanship. Though they obtained their first weaving equipment and designs from their Pueblo teachers, the Navaho soon surpassed the Pueblos in quality of work. The Spanish began to seek Navaho women as slaves to weave for their households, and outlying tribes demanded blankets in trade.

The commercial period, which continues into the present, was thus begun. There are three major divisions of this period: the Golden Age, characterized by the use of red bayeta; the Bosque Redondo and Reservation era; and the Revival.

THE GOLDEN AGE. The reference of Cortez to trade in Navaho blankets shows that by 1799 the commercial period was well under way. Innovations developed, particularly in the use of colors and in such designs as depended largely on color for effect. The Navaho acquired indigo, their first commercial dye, from the Mexicans. The Spanish and Mexicans always had a variety of colors in their woolen materials, whereas the Pueblo weavers, who had pretty vegetable dyes for cotton cloth, were quite conservative in dyeing their wool. The Navaho utilized the knowledge of dyes among their neighbors and experimented further with native plants to discover new dyes which might be adapted to wool.

From 1799 to 1863 the Navaho were prosperous and they spent

A woman's shoulder blanket in white, black, blue, gray, red and orange, produced by a Navajo weaver in about 1880.

18

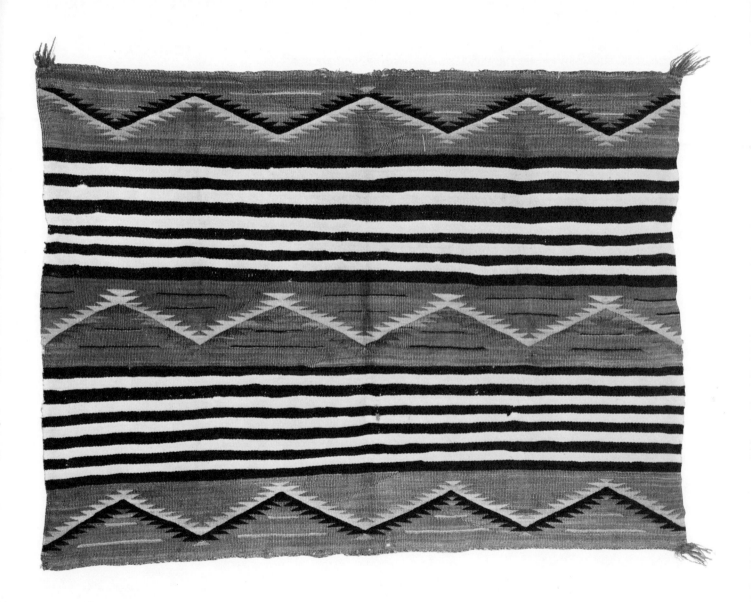

these busy, successful years raiding, farming, herding, and weaving. During the early years of the Golden Age, the Spanish contributed one more item to the prosperity which they had indirectly brought to the Navaho. A common trade article of the time was flannel or baize, generally known in the Southwest by its Spanish name, *bayeta.* The Spaniards bought bayeta in England for trade purposes and for gifts to the Indians. It was made in many glorious colors, but so common and popular was red in the Southwest that red and bayeta have become synonymous to the lay person. About 1800 the Navaho obtained this flannel, which has a long nap on one surface, unraveled the cloth, respun the yarn into a single ply, and wove it into their blankets.

Of the influence of bayeta, Amsden writes (p. 150): "The bayeta period marked the high point, the 'Golden Age' of Navaho weaving, for this rich fabric called forth the best in every phase of the craft—in spinning, dyeing, weaving, pattern creation. Only an expert could wed native wool and bayeta fiber in a harmonious and happy union. Only an artist could realize the full potentialities of such fine smooth wefts, such rich colorings, as bayeta afforded and inspired. And the Navaho woman responded to the stimulus, proved herself an expert and an artist—by grace of bayeta."

The Navaho now had red and blue, in addition to the natural colors of wool, and bayeta red, indigo blue, black, and white were predominant colors for wool. Striped designs continued in popularity, but achieved new interest through the use of red and blue. The conservative Pueblo weaver clung to stripes, but the Navaho craftswoman restlessly experimented with simple geometric patterns and color combinations. She developed the terraced design, which became the most characteristic form of the era between 1800 and

A saddle blanket of unusual design produced circa 1880. Red, blue, yellow and green predominate in the color scheme.

20

1863, just before Kit Carson put a stop to further progress.

The weavers still produced dresses and shirts for tribal use, but to satisfy trade demands they created new styles. Navaho blankets were worn by Indians and white people as far north as the northern Great Plains and as far west as the Pacific. Amsden (p. 206) mentions an engraving of 1822 which shows Indians of the San Francisco Bay region wearing Navaho blankets. The most popular style of garment was the man's shoulder blanket, of which the chief's blanket, with its broad horizontal stripes of black, white, red, and sometimes blue, is a special type.

The *poncho serape* made abundant use of bayeta, and was bought by wealthy Spaniards and the Indians. Essentially it was a blanket, longer than wide, with a slit in the center to slide the garment over the head and around the shoulders. It was sometimes gathered closer to the body by a leather belt ornamented with silver discs, or by a woolen sash. Amsden states (p. 103): "The serape, modified though it has been in many details, must be considered the universal type garment of the Navaho, the type that more than all others is behind the broad phrase 'Indian blanket.' The wealthy tribesman might flaunt his chief's blanket or bayeta poncho, but the humbler men and women of the nation contented themselves with a coarser blanket of similar size and general proportions . . . Burdens of every description, from firewood to babies, were carried in its folds . . . It was a garment by day, a blanket by night, an inseparable companion in all seasons . . . Its form and proportion survive still in the longish-rectangular rugs, five by eight feet or thereabouts in size, which are among the characteristic products of the modern Navaho loom."

This early Hopi-style banded blanket, also shown in the color section, is woven from handspun wool and came off the loom in about 1881 (44" x 62").

BOSQUE REDONDO AND RESERVATION ERA. In 1863 Christopher Carson conquered the Navaho, who were then transferred to Bosque Redondo. The women did very little weaving in captivity and suffered intensely from idleness and inertia. When the Navaho returned in 1868 to their old home, which was now a reservation controlled by the U.S. Government, captivity had reduced them to a "poor white" standard of living, especially in food and clothes. The Government had given them cotton clothing, which gradually came to replace entirely their woolen and buckskin garments. (They had earlier given up wearing their own shoulder blankets because of the weight; a Pendleton blanket was lighter, and when it got wet, it dried quickly.) The flocks upon which the tribe depended for wool had died or been killed. The two sheep per capita granted by the Government to replace the slaughtered stock were insufficient to furnish enough wool for practical purposes. The old market for Navaho blankets had been lost during the absence of the tribe; no longer was there any need to weave them. The tribe was in a sad state.

THE REVIVAL PERIOD. After the return of the Navaho, the Government licensed traders to live on the reservation and barter with the Indians. In this way there was initiated a new era in weaving. Traders Hubbell and Cotton were among the first to see the economic value of blankets in their business. The Navaho had little goods to exchange, and if the making and selling of blankets could be stimulated, the traders would profit both by the sale of these products outside the reservation, and by the sale of goods to the Navaho.

Spectacularly patterned rug at right was purchased in 1893 from a wood-hauler who used it as a seat on his wagon. Colors in the terraced diamond design are black, white, brown, dark blue, green and scarlet.

The effort of Hubbell and Cotton to stimulate the sale of Navaho blankets was very successful. Other traders followed their example, but the lure of easy profits led many, after 1880, to sell aniline dye commercial yarns, like Germantown, and cotton warp to the weavers in order to simplify the work of blanket making and to promote sales. Indeed, they even stipulated the patterns. This resulted in standardization which was alien to the natural versatility and imagination of the weaver. Business boomed until 1900, when the traders and the Navaho weavers discovered that they had defeated their own ends in trying to secure a wide market quickly by lowering the standards of raw material and the workmanship of an article expensive and tedious to produce. Men like Moore, Hubbell, and Fred Harvey realized what was happening, and they urged the weavers to return to their old standards of work, design and colors, and the more careful cleaning and spinning of the wool. They also fought the imitation of Navaho rugs by factories.

To summarize, the revival, dating from 1920, represents a marked effort by associations and traders to encourage the weavers to make again the truly Navaho, geometric designs of strong simplicity in native wool, colored with soft dyes from native plants.

The traders purchased three major types of blankets: heavy, coarse blankets; saddle blankets; and shoulder blankets which were related to the poncho serape of earlier days. Of the blankets which had become rugs, Amsden writes (p. 223): "The Navaho rug came into being because the American demanded a textile meeting his needs and satisfying his graphic concepts; that it retained something (of) the tribal flavor is not due to him but to the weaver, who either could not or would not divest herself completely of her racial individuality."

An early classic Navajo weaving, produced in about 1860, before the internment of the Navajos at Bosque Redondo. White, black and red are used in the color scheme of this blanket.

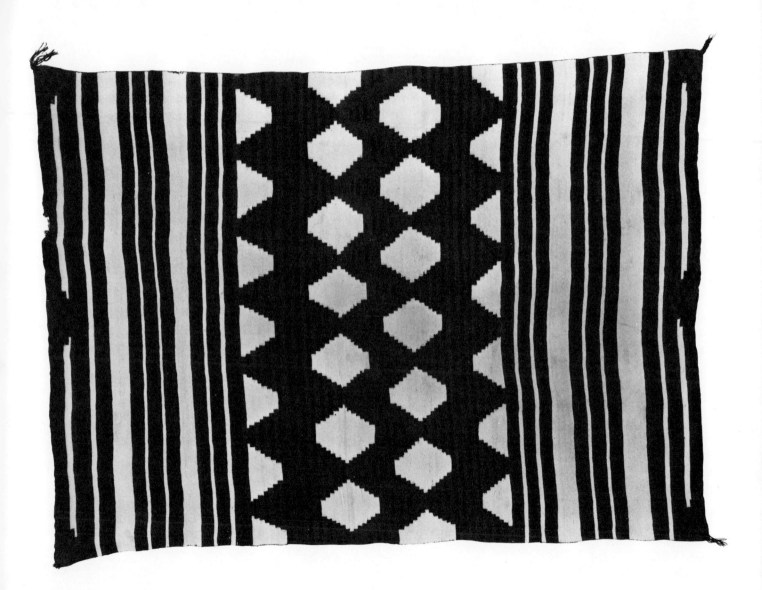

Bayeta had vanished from the scene by 1875. The garish colors of the later day Germantown yarn and the native wool, both dyed with aniline dyes, replaced bayeta. "As the terraced style was characteristic expression of bayeta, so is the diamond of Germantown" (Amsden, p. 213). This pattern was in high favor until 1900, but about 1890 the bordered style had begun to compete with it for popularity. The double-faced blanket, an unusual innovation of this era, never became common.

This post-Redondo period of weaving, which extends into the present, violated almost every tradition and standard of the Navaho weaver. The traditional design, as Amsden (p. 216) points out, has a regular, continuous, and horizontal flow, as if cut from a bolt of cloth; whereas the bordered pattern with a central design and emphasis on vertical figures is alien to Indian craft, though a favorite of the white man. Formerly the Navaho had a religious aversion to bordered patterns because of the weaver's fear of "weaving herself into the blanket" and causing illness. A contrasting line or color which breaks the pattern was left as the road out for the harassed soul. This broken line is also to be seen in pottery and ceremonial baskets which have a zigzag design encircling the upper edge.

In this century experimenting weavers have been making *Yeibichai* blankets which reproduce designs of the sacred sandpaintings and figures of the gods. The Navaho at first objected to the production of these blankets. They have had a good sale, however, so other weavers are suppressing their religious scruples and making the Yeibichai designs. The Navaho have never woven special blankets for ceremonial use. Amsden states (p. 218): "The Navaho blanket . . . never has had a ceremonial or sacred function: the

A classic poncho, in white, blue, green and red (53" x 82"). Several of the rugs shown on these pages were restored by Mabel O'Dell, a master of the specialized craft of rug and blanket repair.

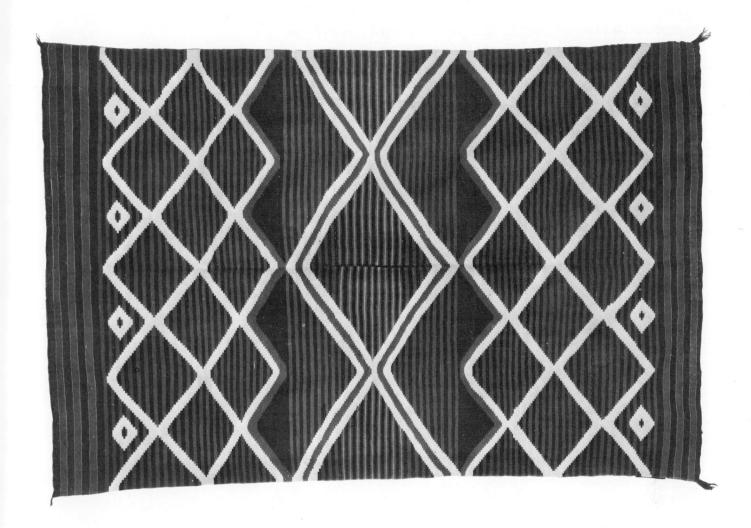

sandpainting, the 'marriage basket,' the dance mask, yes—but not the blanket." Reichard (1936:183) presents a similar view: "The Navajo have kept the symbolic designs of their religion apart, in a separate compartment of their minds, from their ordinary blanket and silverwork patterns. The form occasionally overlaps; the emotions are kept distinct."

The Navaho differ from the Pueblo tribes in that Navaho women, and not men, do the weaving. The only exceptions are the *nadle,* men who are psychically or physiologically peculiar. They have a definite and respected place in the culture and are leaders in artistic work. Navaho legends, in fact, credit them with originating agriculture, basketry, and other crafts.

Practically the entire sheep and weaving industries are controlled by the women. Their husbands and male relatives assist in some of the care of the sheep, but this does not affect ownership. The women own the sheep, select the wool they want for weaving, sell the excess wool and meat, spin the yarn, weave the rugs and sell them.

Weaving is essentially a leisure time activity. Exceptionally artistic weavers may be released from some of the daily chores to devote as much time as possible to their looms. The others weave in winter. In their few spare moments during the busy spring, summer, and fall, they may prefer to do pick-up work like carding, spinning, and dyeing.

Dark red and soft shades of brown prevail in this early pictorial rug from about 1900. Rug features traditional dance figures (60″ x 93″).

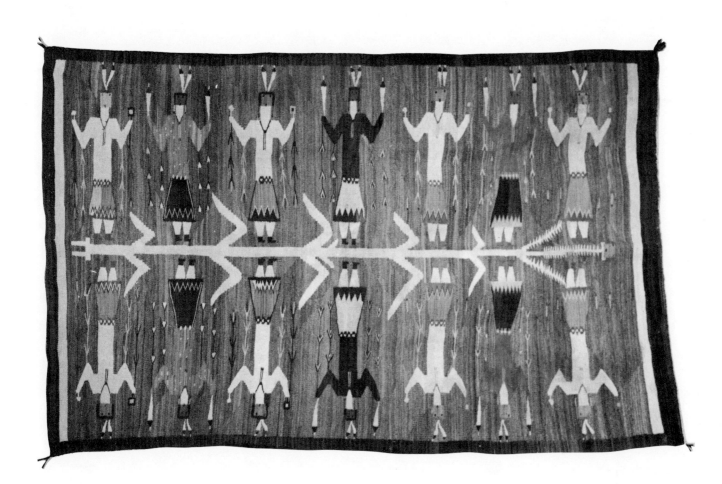

A
PRIMER
OF
NAVAJO
TEXTILES

In discussing Navajo rugs, traders, dealers, and museum people employ terms which refer to the regions in which distinctive styles of weaving are produced, or to particular types of designs in some instances. The designations under which they are listed herein are those now in general use throughout the Southwest. Rugs of these styles are presently available to buyers, especially in trading posts and stores located in the various regions, and in larger establishments where wide selections are offered. Also, some arts and crafts marketing cooperatives are located on the reservation: Canyon de Chelly Association in Chinle, Arizona; Dine Bi Association in Tuba City, Arizona; Four Corners Arts and Crafts Inc., Shiprock, N.M.; and Crown Point Rug Weavers Association in Crown Point, N.M. These are all operated by the Navajo craftsmen who founded them and all excess income after expenses returns to the craftsmen.

These cooperatives also organize rug shows and auctions at Crown Point, Window Rock and in border towns. Recently these shows and auctions have been extended to Albuquerque, Austin, Boston, Philadelphia, San Francisco and Washington, D.C.

Weavers dwelling in localities subject to more than one influence may display their preference for a certain style, may combine features, or may exhibit personal whims. As a result, overlaps occur, and non-traditional expressions may appear.

Absolute perfection will not be found in a Navajo rug. The fact that it is hand-woven presupposes a few slight flaws. Furthermore, taboos exist against making anything perfect. Perfection would

By Dr. Bertha P. Dutton

(Adapted from *Navajo Weaving Today* by Dr. Bertha P. Dutton, published by the Museum of New Mexico Press.)

leave the Navajo weaver with nothing for which to strive. On occasion a line of color will be found broken, or a small bit of color will appear in a place where it seems not to belong in the design.

For those unfamiliar with the standards for judging good Indian rugs, it is suggested that they deal with reputable traders or merchants who sell such products throughout the Southwest.

In selecting a Navajo rug or blanket (the term rug is widely used to include both), take heed of the initial impact made by a specimen which you are viewing. How does this particular example appeal to your eye? If you like it on first sight, the chances are that you will always admire it.

Then, of course, you should give thought as to where and how you will use it. Is the size right? Will the colors and perhaps the design arrangement fit in with your other things? Is the rug straight and the weave good? Finally, what is the cost; can you afford it?

The heavier weaves are suitable for floor coverings, as rugs. These generally come in medium to large sizes.

Saddle blankets, which were made originally for use with riding saddles, were woven in two sizes: the single blanket, about 30 x 30 inches, and the double blanket, approximately 30 x 60 inches. Due to their weight, variety of weaves, and pleasing color arrangements (bright colors were avoided because of their tendency to fade when a horse was hot and sweaty), saddle blankets came to have use also as floor rugs. With this development, the conventional sizes have been adhered to less rigidly.

When softer weaves are produced, they permit a variety of uses, such as bed and sofa coverings, drapes, wall hangings, throws, and the like.

The Western Navajo show a general preference for rugs woven with borders and designed with patterns in black, white, grey, brown, and red. Many people look upon these as "real Navajo," as opposed to the unbordered, light colored rugs of Chinle, Wide Ruin, and adjacent areas.

Most of the Western rugs are made in tapestry weave (essentially a weft technique, with none of the warp showing). Diamond and diagonal twills are made around Tuba City, the Gap, and at Na'ah Tee, north of Holbrook, Arizona.

Many fine rugs are produced in the West, with central designs varying from simple to complex, and often with complicated border patterns along the sides, but not at the ends. Here the so-called "Storm" pattern prevails, making use of some of the sacred elements in the design arragements.

Rugs of the Kayenta region are found from southern Utah to Chilchinbito, and Betatakin to Dinnehotso. Those around Kayenta are characteristically woven of black, grey, and red yarns with white background. A simple motif occurs along each edge, commonly a stepped terrace or serrations on a narrow, black border. The central design is made up of a large, serrated diamond in two or three colors, which is squared off at each end, near the border. The "Storm" pattern is generally popular, and many saddle blankets are made throughout the Kayenta region.

Distinctive weaving style prevails in the Oljato district, northeast of Navajo Mountain in Utah. Around Shonto Springs, a yellow vegetal dye is used, with white, grey and black, and perhaps a touch of red. The corn plant is favored as the central element of design, enclosed by side borders in simple motifs, with narrow end border in black.

Getting closer to Chinle, Kayenta weavers may use native dyes in a variety of design patterns. They make both rugs and saddle blankets. Zoned bands may be varied by the use of wavy stripes, similar to the modern Crystal style, with considerable expanses of white. As is customary with patterned saddle blankets, the same design is repeated in each of the corners, and fringes are attached.

Chinle vegetal dye rugs come from a region extending from Rough Rock, southeast of Kayenta, Arizona, eastward to around Chinle, entrance to the spectacularly beautiful country of Canyon de Chelly and Canyon del Muerto. Rugs from this region are closest to the old banded blankets, stylistically. In fact, they may be considered as representing a continuous development. They are generally without border.

The Chinle designs are usually simple, with stripes or elements combined in bands; they commonly feature a relatively small serrated motif and chevrons. Effective patterns result from the use of white and/or grey with various shades of yellow, green, brown, and rose. Occasionally, sandpainting or *Yei* design adaptations are woven with vegetal dyes.

Knowledge of vegetal dyes had been all but lost by the 1920s. A few Navajo weavers in the Chinle region, however, still remembered the recipes and were induced to make softly colored rugs in old style designs. The late Mary Cabot Wheelwright initiated the idea, and L. H. ("Cozy") McSparron had much to do with bringing back this fine type of Navajo weaving. Public interest, approval, and purchases revived the waning rug industry.

Today, the term "Chinle" is almost synonymous with "vegetable," or, more suitably, "vegetal" dye. Over 250 recipes for making vegetal dyes have been recorded. Some aniline dyes are used in combination with natural or native-dyed yarns.

The Ganado region encircles an area extending from Greasewood (lower Greasewood) and Klagetoh on the south, past Cross Canyon, well to the north of Ganado, Arizona, and takes in Cornfields and Sunrise on the west. It thus lies between the Steamboat and Wide Ruin regions, and close to Nazlini. Ganado itself is about 40 miles north of Chambers on U.S. Highway 66. It was named for the last of the Navajo peace chiefs and twelfth signer of the Treaty of 1868, Ganado Mucho.

One of the early trading posts on the Navajo reservation was established at Ganado, in the mid-1870s. This shortly became the Hubbell post, destined to become the most famous of these enterprises in the Southwest. John Lorenzo Hubbell did much to develop and further the art of Navajo weaving. Large rugs were his specialty. Quality of wool was improved and particular attention given to its cleaning, carding, and spinning. Good Navajo designs were encouraged, with well chosen dyes. The deep, rich red color favored there came to be known as "Ganado red" and its tasteful use has contributed to the attractiveness of rugs from the Ganado region.

Some of the Ganado rugs are woven without borders, in zoned patterns of alternating colors; others feature borders. A general characteristic is the use of red background with black border. Ganado weavers have a fondness for combining red with yellow or orange. Common use is made of various geometric designs, fine lines well spaced and regular, and the "comb" motif. A sandpainting style of the region features the red background, with figures woven with much yellow, blue, black, and white. Only a few of these are now produced. Extensive employment of white has been favored in the Ganado rugs, especially in later times. Attractive saddle blankets are made in the region.

In the Round Rock-Lukachukai region certain picture rug designs have developed. Yei-style rugs are woven with predominating amounts of deep red color. Weavers around Greasewood have developed a characteristic portrayal of Feather People. Figures are woven with bird-form upper bodies and pointed, featherlike lower extremities. The heads of the mythical people show conventionalized human features. Erect feathers are shown as head ornaments. There are other ornaments, such as turquoise ear·drops and shell necklaces with turquoise pendants.

Both natural wool and aniline-dye colors are used. The natural colors consist of black, white, and their combination into warm greys, and brown from brown sheep. The figures are outlined with contrasting colors. Rugs of this nature commonly have narrow borders.

Navajo rugs of Crystal style are woven on the eastern slope of the Chuska Mountains in westernmost New Mexico. The typical Crystal rug of today is very different in design pattern from the "old style" productions. Weaving in that locality received encouragement, about 1896, from J. B. Moore, a trader, who found that Navajo blankets were then a discredited product, undesirable and largely unsaleable.

Improved productions were slowly achieved by introducing new ideas in preparing and dyeing the yarn. At first, wool was sent away for scientific cleaning and preparation for dyeing; this influenced the Navajo weavers to clean their wool thoroughly so that it would take the dyes well. Standards of quality were established. The weavers were shown how to produce grey shades by carding black and white wool together. They were encouraged to weave rugs in black, white, grey, and brown only.

Bordered styles were favored by buyers, and thus they were introduced into Crystal compositions. Red and blues also came to have extensive use in the designs. These rugs became highly desired. Some time after 1912, the Crystal style of rugs faded into oblivion. By the early 1930s, it was said that "one no longer hears mention of the Crystal rug."

During the past few decades, fortunately, Crystal rugs have again come to the fore. They are well woven, generally, with pleasing designs. Horizontal bands in tasteful arrangements, with alternating wavy stripes, have become characteristic. Sometimes, simple decorative units, such as arrows or other motifs, are added to the designs. On occasion, narrow borders frame designs of more elaborate composition, with limited use of the distinctive wavy stripes.

Teec-Nos-Pos rugs are characterized by their decorative technique, primarily one of outline designs. The name, in Navajo, means "circle of cottonwood trees."

During the 1890s, when Germantown yarns in their wide range of colors became available to the Navajo, the serrate design was in high favor. Many weavers were inspired to work several of these gay colors into a single fabric, outlining the zigzags with narrow edgings of contrasting colors. Pleasing results were achieved.

The outlining technique was allowed to lapse for a time. It was

A
SAMPLER
OF
NAVAJO
WEAVING

FOREGROUND: "Storm" pattern bordered rug from 1890-1910 period (49" x 72"). ON THE FIREPLACE: Classic saddle blanket (left) made in mid-nineteenth century (32" x 50"); modern Two Grey Hills style mohair rug (center) typifies the colors, design and fineness of weave of textiles from that region (24" x 30"); Coal Mine Mesa region rug (29" x 59").

ABOVE: Bold stripes and diamonds dominate pattern of this classic "chief" blanket (55" x 65"). A classic woman's dress from the early nineteenth century, in black and bayeta red, lies atop the man's blanket (31" x 49").

LEFT: Post-classic serrate diamond design blanket at left dates from the 1880s, employs Germantown yarn and ravelled flannel (57" x 73"). Classic shoulder blanket of terraced diamond design, at right, dates from 1860-1880 period and was woven from commercial yarns (49" x 72").

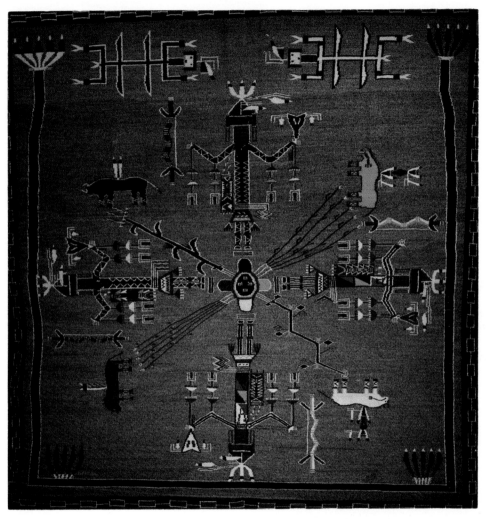

SANDPAINTING IN NAVAJO WOOL. This large graphic rug was made in the early twentieth century and depicts the Plume or Feather Way sandpainting (95" x 99"). The sandpainting rugs do not have ceremonial significance.

ABOVE: Classic ponchos from the mid-nineteenth century, at upper left and right of photo, employ natural white and brown wools, ravelled bayeta flannel for red, and indigo dyed yarn for blue (both ca. 52″ x 84″). Hopi-style banded blanket in lower left, woven from handspun wool, has been repaired by Mabel O'Dell (44″ x 62″).

LEFT: Shoulder blanket of the late terraced style, produced in the 1880s (52″ x 72″).

OPPOSITE PAGE: Fascinating array of colors and designs in rugs from Crystal (N.M.) area, Monticello (Utah), and Kayenta and Chinle areas in Arizona.

COLORS OF NAVAJOLAND. Wedge weave blanket at left was made from handspun wools, some dyed in native dyes and some aniline dyed. It was produced in about 1890. The blanket's soft gray areas are composed of natural white and natural black wool carded together (48" x 71"). A banded saddle blanket is shown at right (31" x 60").

VIBRANT "GERMANTOWN" OF MANY DESIGNS. This is an excellent example of the Navajo rugs woven with Germantown commercial yarns from Pennsylvania. Germantown yarn is four-ply, aniline dyed. Rug was made in the 1890s (37" x 70").

LEFT: Early revival style Navajo textiles were result of efforts of both Indian and trader to restore strong design themes, native wool and natural dyes to Navajo weaving. This finely woven rug features soft colors in its horizontal zoned design (42″ x 67″). RIGHT: Double-faced weave example, produced in 1954, also employs native dyes and natural wool (31″ x 52″).

then re-employed, using fine homespun wool yarns to produce rugs of high quality. This style became popular in the Teec-nos-pos (*T'iisnazbas*)-Biklabito* area, west of Shiprock, New Mexico. It can usually be relied upon that an outline blanket is well woven, for only an accomplished weaver can execute such designs.

Teec-nos-pos rugs, in the many bright colors and designs of today, command a greater price than less complicated productions.

Two Grey Hills rugs are made in the region east of the Chuska Mountains, in western New Mexico, wherein are located the Toadlena (*Toh-ha-lene*), Two Grey Hills, Drolet, and Little Water trading posts. The region lies mostly to the west of U.S. Highway 666, about midway between Shiprock and Gallup, New Mexico.

Prior to 1911, rugs produced in this region were coarse and without distinctive design, woven in natural colors of wool not well cleaned. The Navajo of that area have always had a dislike of red color.

The improvement of weaving in the region may be credited to Ed Davies and George Bloomfield, early operators of the Two Grey Hills and Toadlena trading post, respectively. Although competitors, these two were good friends, and both worked toward the development of better weaving among their weavers. They furthered the use of handspun wool in natural black, white, and brown, and their combination into gray and tan shades; and they

---

* Like most Navajo words, when they are put into English, various spellings appear, *e.g.,* Tees nos pos, Te Nos Pas, Teec nos pas, Tes nos pans; Beclabito, Beklabito, Keklabito.

excluded aniline dyes and the use of Germantown yarns (which were manufactured in Pennsylvania).

An almost standard size of rug (48 inches by 72 inches) was established, with an outside black border two inches wide. Into the latter shortly was introduced the "spirit" trail, or line, such as often appeared in Southwestern pottery and basketry, with the thought of allowing for the escape of any malevolent spirit that some figure might possess.

Certain of the Two Grey Hill weavers are said to have gathered Chaco Black-on-White potsherds from ruin sites, and to have developed geometric designs for their rugs from these.

As in other regions where similar efforts have been made, the quality of the Two Grey Hills rugs slowly improved. By 1925, a distinctive regional style had been developed. Two Grey Hills weaving came to enjoy great fame, based on the modesty and good combination of colors and for perfection of technique. Rarely are other than natural colors used; if they occur, the quantity is small. The yarn is evenly and finely spun, and firmly woven.

Starting with a black border— often borders within borders— compositions are effectively worked out. Design patterns are varied, but they are characterized by geometric compositions made up of many small elements; the arrangement of the design units is balanced and symmetrical. Usually a large, central motif is shown, with little space left unfilled about it. Decorative units include the rhombus with toothed edges, frequently employing small triangles; diagonal bands formed by serrations which are outlined; comb patterns; modified stars, swastikas, (these have been rare since World War II, for the Navajo took note of the non-Indian significance of this symbol); interlocking stepped or recurved frets; triangles, crosses, terraces, diamonds, etc.

Fortunately, those pioneers who started the modern Two Grey Hills development have been followed by other individuals who have continued to encourage the weavers and promote the rugs from that region. Since about 1945, the weaving has been of general excellence. An outstanding weaver of all time is Daisy Taugelche. Her handspun weft threads are so fine that they rarely count less than 90 to an inch, and her superior productions count 110 threads to an inch. They are as soft as cashmere.

Needless to say, Two Grey Hills rugs are the most expensive of all Navajo weaving. Even the small pieces, which are now woven along with larger sizes, carry high prices. The cost of a Two Grey Hills rug is commonly greater than that of a Persian rug.

The San Juan region extends along the San Juan River in northwestern New Mexico, from west of Shiprock to the east of Farmington. There are rugs of both the "regular" and "specialty" patterns, those with native or aniline dyes, and some with combinations of both.

Yei, or *Yeibichei,* rugs originated in the San Juan region about 1900. The designs, usually worked in a plain weave, portray personages who appear in the Navajo ceremonials. They are representations of male and female dancers, primarily, who take part in the Feather Dance, a dramatic feature of the Nightway. The figures are rarely, if ever, conscientious reproductions of Navajo deities. Some weavers using sacred designs seek to avoid disfavor by omitting essential details.

The first rug woven with a Yei design created great furor among the Navajo. It was made by a woman of inventive genius who liked to represent figures, animals and people, and who, being free of the usual superstitions which prevailed, ventured to portray a deific personator and sacred symbols. Finding that the white man favored her production, this weaver turned out one Yei rug after another, in a monotonously standardized pattern. A few other women in the San Juan region wove similarly designed rugs after 1900.

Despite the fact that Yei rugs are much less attractive than the simple designs which are truly representative of Navajo weaving, their strange and esoteric appearance has caused them to be sold, generally, as "extra precious," at high prices. They are no longer rare; instead, they have become rather numerous.

There is a white rug with brightly colored figures which is characteristic of the Shiprock area. The idea was started by a trader there, in the early 1920s. Garish colors often result from injudicious use of aniline dyes. In recent years, some use of vegetal dyes has been made in producing pictorial designs, primarily adaptations of Yei or sandpainting motifs. Some use of cotton warp is employed in such representations.

Mohair yarns were put into use during the 1930s, first, in saddle blankets. This resulted in combinations of quiet colors with softness of texture. However, the tendency of such blankets to slide rendered them more ornamental than practical. Mohair is also difficult to spin.

Sandpainting rugs should not be confused with the so-called Yeibichei, or Yei, rugs. The first sandpainting rug is said to have been woven in 1919, by a Navajo medicine man, who made use of the whirling logs pattern of the Yeibichei or Nightway. Later, he gave his designs to two of his nieces. On rare occasions, other medicine men have produced sandpainting rugs. It is only when a faithful depiction of a complete sandpainting is rendered that such a rug can be considered a copy of a sandpainting. The Navajo people do not like such rugs. In general, they believe weaving of this nature to be a misuse of power, and therefore dangerous.

Following the original productions, numerous imitations have come onto the market. Since no soft colors in yarn can duplicate the earth-colored sands of authentic sandpaintings, the rugs of this style are commonly garish. Aniline dyes are used for the intense colors. Some weavers of sandpainting designs seek to avoid ill favor by omitting traditional details. Certain ones make use of cotton warp, thus lessening the value, even though the weaving is perhaps good and the design attractive. In some areas, superior weaving is demonstrated. Because of their quaintness of style, rugs with sandpainting designs have intrigued the white buyers, who have created a demand for them. It must be understood that the majority of sandpainting rugs are actually curios made for the non-Indian trade. They have no cultural significance in Navajo life.

An old type which has seen continued production all over the Navajo country is the so-called "Chief" blanket. These were made for shoulder robes and, as such, are woven crosswise instead of lengthwise. Wrapped around the body broadside, they show off the stripes to good advantage.

Tradition prescribes the colors and design, the wide, alternating stripes of black and white, the use of blue, and the pattern. In the blankets of accomplished weavers, the lines of the design remain true when folded in from the corners, and then folded again.

The value of rugs of this type caused them to be restricted, in former days, to those of wealth and affluence, such as the headmen or "chiefs"of other than Navajo Indians, especially the Plains tribes—and thus the nomenclature. Only a very few blankets of this style are now woven in the San Juan region, or elsewhere.

The Gallup region takes in considerable territory in each direction from that western New Mexico town, wherein a great many small pieces of weaving, called "throws," are produced. These are loosely woven, usually with cotton warp, and are consequently cheap in comparison with well-woven rugs.

The region is especially recognized for a variety of saddle blankets, in all the known weaves of the Navajo. Saddle blankets generally show a different patterning from that of other Navajo blankets. Aside from the plain weave, there are "speckled" patterns, diagonal twill (also called "braided")—which affords the greatest scope for design ideas (herringbone, zigzags, diamonds, broken diamonds, wedges, "lightning,"etc.)--tufting,and double-face weaving.

Double-face blankets never have been popular with Navajo weavers, although they are known back to 1885. They are always considered unique, and have no aboriginal American precedent. It is believed that the Navajo devised this technique from observation of a commercial fabric. It has been noted that the machine-made, figured Pendleton blanket, now so widely used by the Navajo, is a counterpart of the double-faced Navajo production.

Usually, double-face rugs are made with ordinary weave on one side and a banded pattern on the contrasting side. If a complicated pattern is woven on the back, it has to be done "blindly," for it cannot be seen by the weaver.

A nicely designed Navajo rug or blanket, well woven of good materials, will be a lifelong possession, given reasonable care. This is another point in favor of choosing wisely.

The longer the non-Navajo buyers continue to demand fine examples of this indigenous art, the longer will its production continue. Machine-made articles can never give satisfaction equal to that resulting from ownership of beautiful hand-wrought pieces which reflect something of the true American culture.

WEAVING A NAVAJO RUG

By Josephine Wapp

The loom which the Navajos presumably copied from the Pueblos is a homemade affair, which differs from other looms in having no permanent framework. Weaving a rug consumes the loom, and a new one has to be made for every piece of work. Only the supporting poles and the weaving implements can be used again and again.

The loom is upright, tightly stretched between two stout poles. The weaver lays the warp in a continuous line from pole to pole while these lie on the ground. After they are raised to the upright position and pulled tight, the heddles, controlled by loops of string clasping alternate warps, are attached.

Weaving begins at the bottom, with a strand of weft carefully passed through an opening in the warp track made by turning the batten sideways in the opened shed. Then the batten is turned edgeways and used to press the warp strand into place. A new shed is opened by pulling forward the heddle rod. The batten holds it open, and a fresh strand is inserted. A wooden comb with a handle is also used to press the weft in place.

Preparation of the raw wool involves several processes: shearing, cleaning, carding and spinning. The spinner twirls her wooden spindle with the right hand while the left manipulates the wool being wound around it. Several separate spinnings are needed to produce a strand of even average fineness.

A Navajo rug is made up of three types of yarn: the warp, the weft, and the edging cord. The warp, a thin, tightly-spun yarn, is

Josephine Wapp, a former teacher of traditional weaving techniques at the Institute of American Indian Arts, demonstrates the time-honored use of the upright loom common to all Navajo weaving.

51

initially strung on the loom. It has inherent strength as it must be able to withstand great tension; the weft, a larger fluffier yarn, is woven between the stretched warp so as to completely cover it in a tapestry weave. It is this yarn that is responsible for the beautiful texture of Navajo rugs; the edging cord, a two-ply hand spun yarn, is used on the ends and sides of the rug in the selvage position, to increase wearability.

All yarns contain much of the natural sheep oil, which largely accounts for the durability and resilience for which Navajo rugs are known. The lanolin content also provides some resistance to soiling. Navajo warp is spun thin and tight. The tightness must supply both strength and resistance to abrasion caused by the wooden comb.

When commercial yarns are used instead of Navajo handspuns, the best substitute is a strong, fine tightly spun product available through commercial yarn companies. Another good substitute is a four-ply mohair, or camel hair, which is available in a variety of natural colors. Also suitable and available is a Mexican handspun warp yarn. It is strong, single-ply, and similar to that of the Navajo. A respun worsted wool carpet warp may also be used.

Some of the Navajo weavers use a cotton warp, at the expense of the rug's durability. This carpet warp is available in several different sizes.

The main criteria in the selection of handspun yarns are not only the color relationships, but also the uniformity of size and twist between colors. Using large and small yarns, or tightly and loosely spun yarns, in the same rug causes rows to be uneven,

Ella Mae Sandoval from the Cuba, N.M., region demonstrates the carding process: Wool is positioned on the carder in photo at top. Proper hand position while carding is shown below.

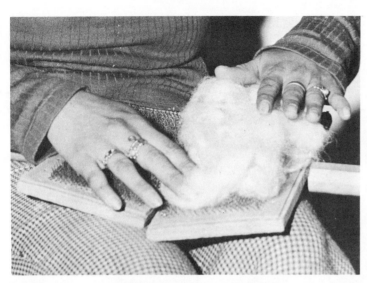

Spinning wool into yarn with the ancient hand spindle, still used by many Navajo weavers. Spindle is operated by student Cecelia Sandoval.

stripes to wiggle across the rug, and the weaving line to have high and low areas which demand constant adjustment.

Commercially spun yarns are readily available, some of which are single-ply and have the quality of handspun. Most, however, cause a sacrifice in the lovely handspun texture of the final product. One of the positive features of the commercial yarn is that you are assured of all colors being the same weight, size, and twist. Rug wool is the most common commercial substitute. Since so many weights are available, and the size affects the warp, setting the size of the weft used determines the spacing of the warp.

The edging cord is a two-ply yarn which is made from the regular weft. The color is determined by the color of the weft at the

Opening shed on the upright loom. Melba Largo of Gallup, N.M., shows how it's done.

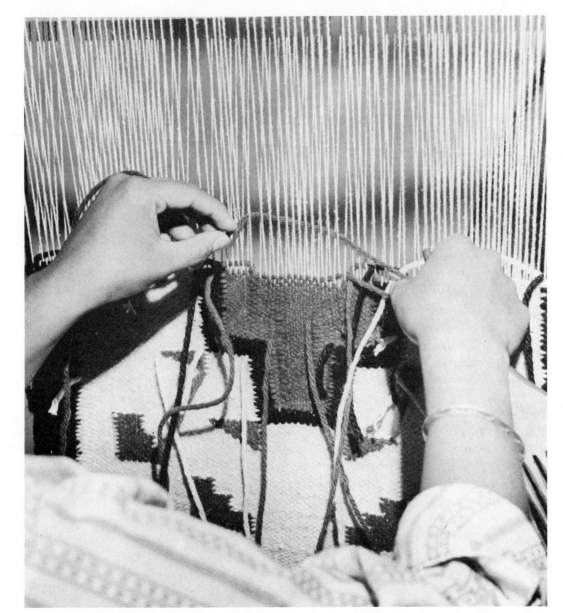

Melba Largo here weaves part of a
terraced pattern in the traditional
Navajo manner.

bottom and top of the weaving. The two should match, or at least blend, unless a decorative contrast is desired. To make the edging cord, one has to respin doubled yarns tightly on a spindle in a direction opposite to the initial spin, then submerge the wool in water until it is thoroughly wet, and stretch it tightly to dry. When the yarn is dry, the spin is set, and the yarn is removed and wound into a ball ready for use.

Color was perhaps the hardest problem the Navajo weaver had to solve, for of course she would never rest content to work in the restricted color range of natural white and rusty brown-black wools. Pueblo experience in native dyestuffs certainly was of some help, but dyes provided by the Spanish settlers were the most useful. One was an excellent red, this being the hardest color to create with any of the natural resources of the Navajo country. It came as a cloth ready dyed, imported from Europe, and called in Spanish *bayeta.* The clever Navajos raveled it down to its individual threads, and retwisted them two or three together to make a strand of weft to combine with the coarser strands of their own spinning.

Blue ranked next to red, which the Spanish traders supplied in the form of lump indigo from Mexico.

The rest of the colors were entirely native to the country. A beautiful sunny yellow was achieved by boiling the flowers of rabbit brush, with a lump of alum as a mordant to make the color fast. The addition of fresh leaves and twigs of the same plant gave a greenish tone to this dye. The roots of the *canaigre,* rich in tannin, yielded a brownish extract which gave a rich orange tone to white wool without requiring any mordant. Black was obtained by a complicated process of combining yellow ocher and piñon gum

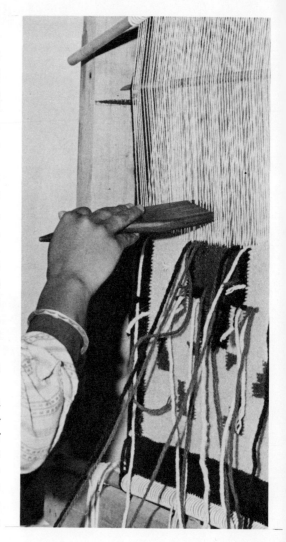

with leaves of sumac. Other popular natural dye materials used today are Indian tea, onion skins, and juniper berries.

But when the traders brought in commercial dyes, so that the weaver could empty a simple little envelope of powder into boiling water and get a whole bucketful of vivid color, natural dyes began to be neglected. The new colors were not so harmonious or pleasing as the old. As the demand for rugs grew however, certain traders encouraged their best weavers to take the trouble to gather the plant materials in proper season and patiently make the old native dyes.

Traditional Navajo designs are handed down from generation to generation, with some innovation by each weaver. As a result, some rug designs have reached a certain refinement and precision of balance, color, and proportion. The refinement of a rug design is possible only by repetition over time. From watching grandmother do it, then mother, and then doing it oneself, the design becomes memorized, usually by string count.

In Navajo rug weaving, the tools are basic, the process rhythmic, and the whole weaver-loom relationship a very natural one.

Beating the weft with a comb. A quality Navajo rug has a tight, durable weave.

RESTORING
NAVAJO
BLANKETS

By Sally and Lisa Kandarian

Collectors from all over the world seek out Mabel O'Dell to restore life to old and priceless examples of the Navajo weaver's art. Duplicating the wool, the dyes, and the particular spin is a remarkable art in itself.

Mabel O'Dell is not a Navajo Indian, but stored in her head over the years is more knowledge and awareness of the structure of wools and construction of rugs than most weavers gather in a lifetime. Mrs. O'Dell's business is restoring the work of other weavers' hands. Weaving a Navajo rug is a complicated process, starting with shearing of sheep and emerging only much later as a finely crafted object of art. To take an old rug or blanket, analyze the type of wool used, the dye used, and how it was spun is the job Mabel undertakes before she even contemplates the mechanical problems of how to reweave the ruined spot.

For Mabel this almost unique occupation began in Taos in about 1923. Then as now many people had Navajo weaving which needed repair for one reason or another, from old museum pieces with gaping holes to everyday frayed edges. There was no one around who would take the time and effort to do a decent job, so Mabel set out to teach herself, so that she could repair rugs for a trader friend. Over the years, as her skill and knowledge grew, her reputation spread. During the W.P.A. period she spent three years on a project at the Laboratory of Anthropology in Santa Fe, working under Dr. Harry P. Mera restoring rugs and blankets in the Laboratory collection. Now as she sits in her sunny room working at the big table on rollers (so she can get to all sides of the rug) she reminisces about requests from museums and collectors all over

The O'Dell home and workshop is an old railroad depot, moved from the town of Cerrillos to a small hamlet near Albuquerque.

the world, requests to bring back to life old, unique and priceless examples of the Navajo art.

Mabel O'Dell lives with her husband Clayton in the Cerrillos railroad station, still painted bright yellow and still proclaiming CERRILLOS on the ends even though it has taken root in a tiny hamlet southeast of Albuquerque. In the yard, out by the garage-tool shed, a swing hangs from the branch of an old cottonwood, not for the grandchildren but for Mr. O'Dell, who happens to like to swing once in a while. Inside is a very snug and cosy abode. The living room has as its focal point the south bay where Mabel works at the big table, spinning wheel and tool bench, with sacks of wool and all kinds of scraps and pieces from old rugs and wool garments.

When they lived in Cerrillos, Mabel raised her own sheep because she had difficulty matching yarns with fleece available commercially. She discovered that jet black wool is found on yearling caracul lambs, and that this long fibered wool could be used to match merino. She experimented with cross breeding to increase her selection of textures and colors in the fleece. With various black sheep and white sheep she was able to match all the whites, blacks and grays that a Navajo weaver could devise.

Mabel, however, didn't follow the traditional style in the washing of the fleece. She used detergent instead of yucca root. Instead of gathering the yucca and pounding the root to make soap, Mabel says "I'd better be fixin' the hole!"

Sheep raising is no longer a part of Mabel's life, but she goes to the dye pot when she needs a color match, either starting from white or bringing out or toning down an established color. This is perhaps the most difficult part of the process because if the wool is dyed so it will match the older work, it will fade and in time become obvious. Mabel said that she used to do more dyeing, but that now she only does it as a last resort if she can't find an old scrap to match.

Colored wools can be carded with white or with a modifying color to achieve a perfect match. She also has success with raveling fabrics made of handspun, and in some cases, commercially spun wool. Over the years Mabel has accumulated bags and bags of scraps, some of very old bayeta pieces from Europe. These bayeta yarns were used by the Indians who raveled the cloth, respun the

Mrs. O'Dell spinning at the "marvelous machine," her homemade spinning wheel. Her husband fashioned the device from a bicycle wheel and other salvaged parts.

yarn and wove it into extremely fine blankets in the early part of the 19th century. Mabel keeps any likely looking scrap, knowing that it could be years before she might need to use it. Highly prized also are scraps of old indigo wools and the various vegetable dyes. The texture and sheen of an old piece of wool is something almost impossible to match with new wool, no matter how skilled the

66

Here the renowned craftswoman is shown carding wool with her favorite Mexican carders. She feels that manual ones such as these work best.

dyer and spinner. On top of her tool bench Mabel has a rotary drum carding machine, but she finds that very fine wool carders which come from Scandinavia, New England or, in the case of her favorite ones, Mexico, seem to work out best.

Mabel discovered early on that the only way to mend Navajo weavings was to learn to spin, which she did in Ranchos de Taos.

"There was a school there that was teaching the kids how to spin. I spun with a top; it was the only way I knew how, then," she says. She spun with a top for years, always wanting a spinning wheel but never finding just what she wanted. Finally she called upon her husband who said,"Well, if you just want something to work with, I can fix you up something you can work with." That was some 30 years ago and the wheel he built out of a table, a bicycle wheel, a child's wagon wheel and some scrap angle iron does the job perfectly. She says it has lanolin all over it "til it is just slick." The long piece of iron left on the spindle shaft became a useful tool for unwinding the yarn and then twisting it into the two-ply whippings used around the edges of rugs and blankets. The wheel has enough momentum so that Mabel can spin out a long thread, backing away from the wheel while it spins.

Having achieved the perfect mending yarn, Mabel now sets herself to the task of reconstruction. Her tools for doing this are many

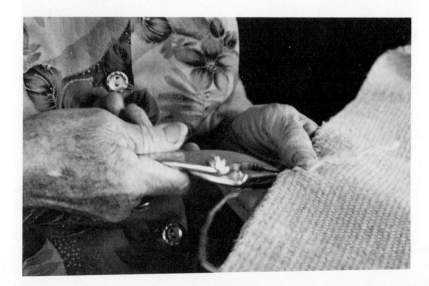

Mabel O'Dell has found that a pair of pliers is useful in tightening the weave of an old Navajo rug. The work is a labor of love for Mrs. O'Dell, who has been restoring treasures like this one for more than fifty years.

and varied and she keeps them handy on an old dresser in her workroom. She carefully matches each thread of warp and weft working the new into the old so that it cannot be seen. "Oh, that hole! Even the littlest hole—I have to restore each beautiful weaving just the way it was."

Testimonial to her craft can be found in many private and museum collections, but now she is semiretired and only takes on special jobs, old and valuable weavings which should be restored as historic objects. Al Packard accepts a few jobs for her at his trading post in Santa Fe. Others come from collectors, some wise and some lucky. Mabel showed us a fantastic blanket sent by a man who had picked it up at an auction in Kansas, not really knowing what it was.

Mabel O'Dell's craft is one of infinite love and patience, just as is the craft of the Navajo weaver.

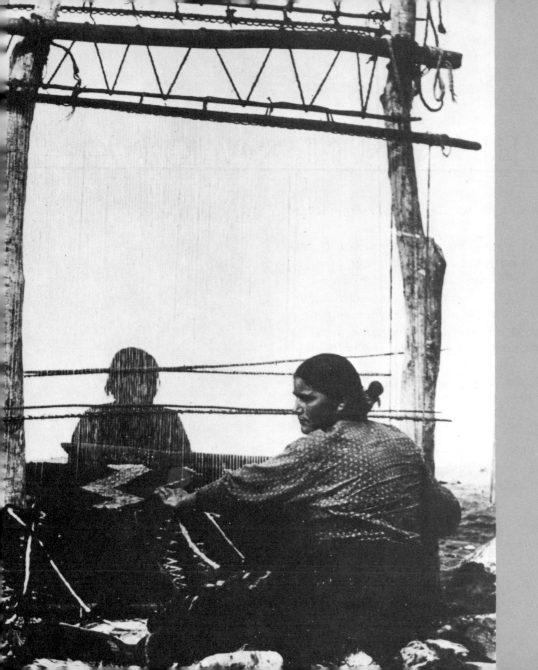

HOW TO TELL A GENUINE NAVAJO RUG

HOW TO TELL A GENUINE NAVAJO RUG

"Beware of fakes and imitations" caution several recent articles referring to Mexican-made replicas of Navajo rugs. So well-copied and uniformly woven are these imitations that they are easily mistaken by the unsuspecting buyer for genuine Navajo rugs.

Reputable dealers, many of whom have been in the business of selling Indian crafts for years, speak frankly of their bewilderment. Since most are not experienced in the technique of weaving, they frequently find it difficult to distinguish the imitation from the real. Some stores do not even try, perhaps not suspecting the ruse, perhaps not caring.

Even more disturbing is the trader who specifically seeks the low-cost Mexican product because it sells quicker than the better-made, higher priced Navajo especially to the tourist looking for a bargain.

Adding to the confusion are Navajos themselves. Some bring an imitation to the trader and claim it as their own work. The trader who might be suspicious of an article sold by a non-Indian is often off guard in such a situation.

It is in response to this generally frustrating and irritating situation that this method of differentiation is offered.

By Noel Bennet

(Adapted from *Genuine Navajo Rug–Are You Sure?* by Noel Bennet, published jointly by the Museum of Navaho Ceremonial Art and the Navajo Tribe.)

TWO QUICK TESTS TO CHECK WHETHER A RUG IS NAVAJO OR MEXICAN:

POSITION RUG VERTICALLY

Test no. 1: EXAMINE SIDES. Slide yarn apart at sides; if multiple warp clusters are present, the rug is MEXICAN.

Test no. 2: EXAMINE TOP AND BOTTOM. Slide yarn apart an inch from top and bottom; alternate triple and single warps which terminate in fringe-ends indicate that the rug is MEXICAN.

See illustrations on the following two pages ⟶

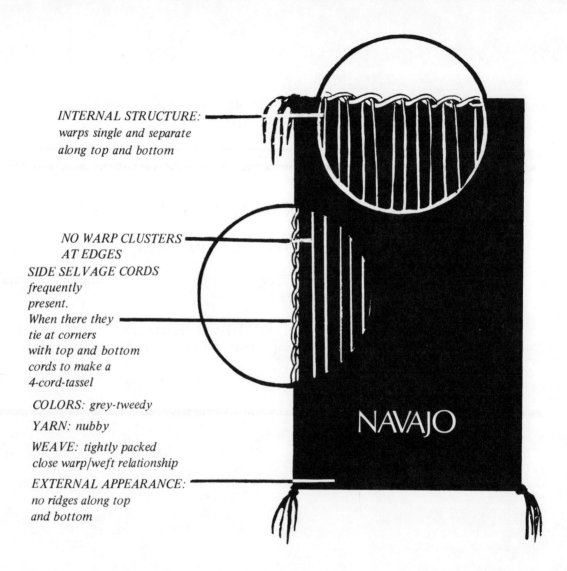

INTERNAL STRUCTURE:
warps single and separate
along top and bottom

NO WARP CLUSTERS
AT EDGES
SIDE SELVAGE CORDS
frequently
present.
When there they
tie at corners
with top and bottom
cords to make a
4-cord-tassel

COLORS: grey-tweedy

YARN: nubby

WEAVE: tightly packed
close warp/weft relationship

EXTERNAL APPEARANCE:
no ridges along top
and bottom

NAVAJO

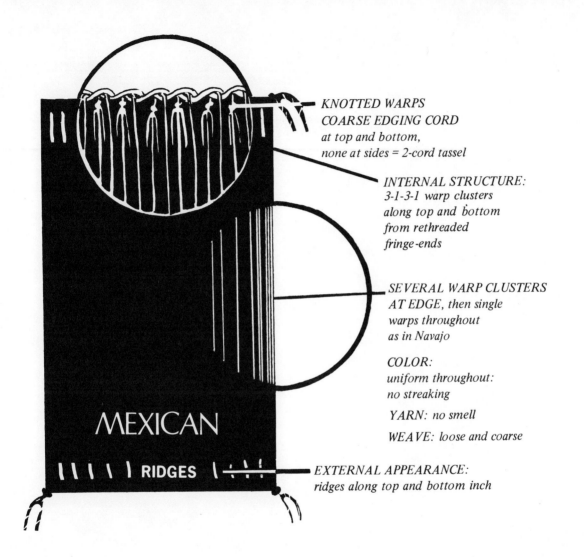

KNOTTED WARPS
COARSE EDGING CORD
*at top and bottom,
none at sides = 2-cord tassel*

INTERNAL STRUCTURE:
*3-1-3-1 warp clusters
along top and bottom
from rethreaded
fringe-ends*

SEVERAL WARP CLUSTERS
AT EDGE, *then single
warps throughout
as in Navajo*

COLOR:
*uniform throughout:
no streaking*

YARN: *no smell*

WEAVE: *loose and coarse*

MEXICAN

RIDGES

EXTERNAL APPEARANCE:
ridges along top and bottom inch

SUGGESTED READING

Amsden, Charles Avery
    1934   *Navaho Weaving, Its Technic and History.* The Fine Arts Press, in cooperation with the Southwest Museum, Santa Ana, California (Peregrine Smith, Inc. edition, 1975).

Arizona Highways
    1974   *Special Edition: Southwest Indian Weaving.* Vol. 50, No. 7. Phoenix.

Bennett, Noel, and Tiana Bighorse
    1971   *Working with the Wool: How to Weave a Navajo Rug.* Northland Press, Flagstaff.

Cerny, Charlene
    1975   *Navajo Pictorial Weaving.* Museum of New Mexico Press, Santa Fe.

Dedera, Don
    1975   *Navajo Rugs: How to Find, Evaluate, Buy and Care for Them.* Northland Press, Flagstaff.

Dutton, Bertha
    1975   *Navajo Weaving Today* (Revised Edition). Museum of New Mexico Press, Santa Fe.

Franciscan Fathers
    1910   Weaving. In *An Ethnological Dictionary of the Navaho Language,* pp. 221-225. St. Michaels, Arizona.

James, George Wharton
    1914   *Indian Blankets and Their Makers.* A. C. McClurg and Co., Chicago.

Matthews, Washington
  1884   Navajo Weavers. *Third Annual Report, Bureau of American Ethnology,* pp. 371-391. Washington.
Mera, H. P.
  1947   *Navajo Textile Arts.* Laboratory of Anthropology, Inc., Santa Fe. (Peregrine Smith, Inc. edition, 1975).
Reichard, Gladys A.
  1936   *Navajo Shepherd and Weaver.* J. J. Augustin, Publisher, New York.
Wheat, Joe Ben
  1976   Spanish American and Navajo Weaving, 1600 to Now. In *Collected Papers in Honor of Marjorie Ferguson Lambert.* Papers of the Archaeological Society of New Mexico: 3, A. H. Schroeder, ed. Albuquerque Archaeological Society Press, Albuquerque.
Young, Stella
  1940   *Navajo Native Dyes, Their Preparation and Use* (Recipes formulated by Nonabah G. Bryan, drawings by Charles Keetsie Shirley). Indian Handcrafts: 2. U.S. Office of Indian Affairs, Washington.

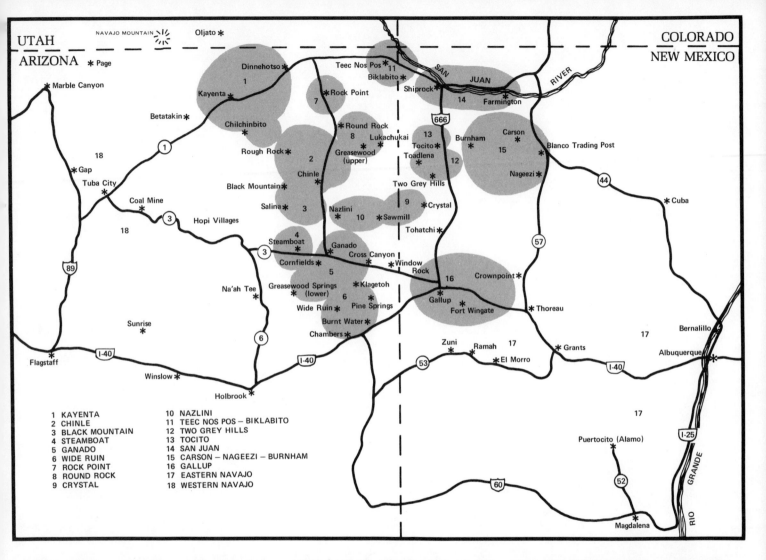

RUG WEAVING REGIONS OF NAVAJOLAND

UTAH
ARIZONA
COLORADO
NEW MEXICO

NAVAJO MOUNTAIN

Oljato
Page
Marble Canyon
Dinnehotso
Teec Nos Pos
Biklabito
Shiprock
SAN JUAN RIVER
Farmington
Kayenta
Betatakin
Rock Point
666
Chilchinbito
Round Rock
Carson
Blanco Trading Post
Gap
Lukachukai
Tocito
Burnham
Tuba City
Rough Rock
Greasewood (upper)
Toadlena
Nageezi
Cuba
Coal Mine
Chinle
Two Grey Hills
44
Black Mountain
Hopi Villages
Salina
Nazlini
Crystal
Na'ah Tee
Sawmill
Tohatchi
57
Steamboat
Ganado
Cross Canyon
Window Rock
Crownpoint
Cornfields
Greasewood Springs (lower)
Klagetoh
Gallup
Thoreau
Sunrise
Wide Ruin
Pine Springs
Fort Wingate
Bernalillo
Burnt Water
Zuni
Ramah
Grants
Albuquerque
Flagstaff
Chambers
El Morro
I-40
Winslow
53
I-40
Holbrook
I-25
Puertocito (Alamo)
RIO GRANDE
60
52
Magdalena

1 KAYENTA
2 CHINLE
3 BLACK MOUNTAIN
4 STEAMBOAT
5 GANADO
6 WIDE RUIN
7 ROCK POINT
8 ROUND ROCK
9 CRYSTAL
10 NAZLINI
11 TEEC NOS POS – BIKLABITO
12 TWO GREY HILLS
13 TOCITO
14 SAN JUAN
15 CARSON – NAGEEZI – BURNHAM
16 GALLUP
17 EASTERN NAVAJO
18 WESTERN NAVAJO

THE WINNING REGIONS OF NAVAJOLAND